The Whispers Of Hearts

A Love Euphoria

Ranya Srivastava

BookLeaf
Publishing

India | USA | UK

Made with ❤ on the BookLeaf Publishing Platform
www.bookleafpub.in
www.bookleafpub.com

Dedication

The love that feels like poetry.

Preface

For the past 3 years, poetry has been my safe haven where my thoughts and feelings had a way of being heard even when I couldn't say them out loud. As a teenage girl, I have experienced the rollercoaster of emotions, have fallen in love with ideas, people, moments, and even situations.

This book is a poetic storyline of me learning to navigate through those unspoken feelings. I never wrote these with the intention of sharing them but I feel in some way it would help others to deal with similar conflicting emotions and also give me a comfort of not being alone.

This is my first step as a poet being unafraid to be vulnerable with her words. So, to whoever is reading, I hope these poems speak to you and if not a lot, just make you feel seen because I believe that words have a way of connecting us. Thank you for choosing this book and I hope you see a reflection of yourself in it.

Acknowledgements

To the love that sparked these verses, people who cheered me on, and the readers who make poetry eternal.

1. Echoes of A New Trust

I used to give it all
thousand reminders a day
I used to show my love
hoping they would stay

no one did, though
left without a word
no explanations given
as I sat with my vision blurred

I went numb, for a while at least
I stopped pouring myself out
I just felt empty
nothing to be angry about

then you came along
you matched the guy in my head
the one I made scenarios with
before sleeping, lying in my bed

I wasn't ready to trust
to open my heart again
but talking to you,
I should be glad for the confidence I gained

I said it, doesn't matter how terrified I was
my brain went, "he could never feel the same"
I'll just say it and
we will never talk about it again

if I saw myself right now
after I know how that went
I would throw a brick at my face
and delete all the poetic love letters sent

because let's be honest
I still am terrified
everything I do reminds me
of the last many times I cried

2. Serendipitous

She didn't like him
She just liked the way he talked
She said she didn't care
But every argument, she lost

She said she'd never fall
For a footballer again
But when he matched her ideas
She thought maybe he'd be worth the pain

She didn't like him
She just liked the way he played
He had everything she liked in a guy
But she knew, for each other, they weren't made

No, she didn't like him
He was annoying after all
What he didn't know was,
How hard she would fall

She'd never admit it though
She hated him, atleast that's what she said
But everytime his name popped up
There wasn't any restraint

Ofcourse she would fall though
Enemies to lovers was her favorite trope
It's just, he didn't know they were enemies
So maybe there was still hope

3. Romantic Fraternization

I hate enemies to lovers
but that's kind of a lie
because I don't like how you counter my words
which kind of makes you my dream guy

You're just so amazing
it annoys me to my core
because when I want to focus
you shout "SCORE!"

You're right, you did score
you bagged a perfect ten
she's just a different kind
other than the ruckus in her head, she's a gem

We're not even enemies
we're something less than friends
and the way you match my energy
it's irritating but worse when it ends

Falling for you? Never.
what kind of a stupid question is that?
because if I ever let myself admit it
I swear my pride shield would crack

But you're kind of my dream guy
he's funny like you
he says the perfect things
as if right on cue

I like you, there, I said it
but you definitely knew
still I'll pretend you don't
so I can lower my hopes for you

You know I hate enemies to lovers
but the lovers part I'd like
because when she says "I hate you"
his heart breaks as if caught in a genocide

4. Concurrence

There's this guy i like
I don't know much about him
but i know he could never fall for me
he's like the oceans and I don't know how to swim

So i happily drown
what i feel confuses me
because the way he talks makes me overthink
and I don't know if it's just friends, he wants to be

Sometimes I think maybe something more
then curse myself for it
because he might be the perfect guy
but I'm not sure I'm the perfect fit

I hate the way crushes work
I just want to read their minds instead
because maybe he likes me
but i can't confirm it just yet

Its funny to even think about
I probably don't even cross his mind
while I lose mine, leaving my heart
in the hope for him to find

I really do hope he does
because I want to hear him yap
just talk about what he loves
even if its just a trap

5. Unnerved

I like you
but i don't tell you that today
maybe i will, in a few years
when i have nothing left to say

I've been writing about you too much
and its only been a few weeks
I pretend to be "cool"
but maybe I'm just one of the geeks

You would never talk to me
if you ever found out I wrote about you
I have confessed so many times
but you just stand there without a clue

Its kind of frustrating
but weirdly relieving too
because I know you'd never like me
still I'm not ready to hear it from you

A few years later, we never even dated
so it might be wrong to say
your favourite song came on
and I regretted not telling you that day

I don't want to experience that feeling
it's just I don't know what else to do
I want to vocalize how I feel
but on what basis would I say that to you?

So I write poems instead
I try not to be too obvious
though I'm sure you have an idea
even if you don't think I'm serious

6. Agitation

God, I like you
so damn much, it hurts
I love talking to you
being a pair of clueless flirts

We're hopeless
one second i think you're falling
the next one, i doubt myself
then my eyes light up,
when i see you calling

We have so much in common,
but I'm sometimes scared,
we might run out of things to talk about
then I'll realise maybe you never cared

You don't judge me when
I say "i like mine obsessed"
I think it all up and
wonder if I'm just trapped in my head

I might be oblivious
my friends say, you're flirting
I say you're just friendly
as if self asserting

But mostly its just me
convincing myself
because I'll be damned
if you ever feel the way i felt

7. Hope

I wanted to be friends with you
I still want to be your friend
but I don't think it was fair
when my feelings wanted our "just friendship" to end

I had these dreams
they weren't holy to say the least
but when I talked to you again
the thoughts suddenly ceased

It wasn't long before I was counting days,
moments, before you changed your mind
because there is this stupid thing called hope
that keeps saying, love, I might find

So I find myself laying awake
I'm emptying out people's opinions of me that I don't
know
"I'm pretty, I'm smart" they say
wondering where my thoughts are supposed to go

Then I think about how it would be,
and if you feel the same as well
because the way you talk gets me wondering
if you too, for me, fell

I say I know nothing could ever happen
because our relation is a little messed
but that stupid hope keeps me going
hoping you won't be like the rest

You never asked me
but I wanted us together
now I'm left thinking
if you could be my "someone better"

8. Love

They say, love,
it's messy and intense
but what about the times
when the calm makes perfect sense?

We're not calm, not at all,
we are the definition of messy
but would it be wrong to say
maybe I like all the guessing?

I know i shouldn't but I'm used to it,
it takes time to trust,
first the uncertainty sets in
as I watch us turn into dust

You don't believe it
and I think where's the flaw
you're the perfect person
I would fill pages, if I could draw

So I'll imagine we fell in love
met under the moonlight
I'll make the most of it
before you're nowhere in sight

But I'll remember you
how could i not?
no matter where i am
you're the only one to be thought

I long to look at you
I could write so much more
but i think I'll scare you away
and talking to me would just be a chore

I know I shouldn't write this
I know its wrong
I'm falling and I'm terrified
because maybe I'm not that strong

9. Reassurance

I hope you meet yourself one day
and realise you're the best to be around
that as soon as you leave the room
it misses your laugh's sound

It misses your presence
the way you talk
every little smile
and even the times you felt distraught

I think it might be obvious
but the "room" is me
when i talk to you
all i want, is for you to feel free

I'm afraid to love again
because I'm afraid, you too might leave
but the promise i made to myself
was "in love I'll always believe"

I want you to as well
if you just give it a chance
I'll reassure you
with my every glance

I know its hard to understand
but I'm trying my best
if you just let me in
I promise, i won't be like the rest

10. Smitten

I don't need the grand gestures
or the loud things
the big moments
that are usually seen

I just want to be known
as yours and you as mine
closest in hearts
even if apart in time

The distance feels too much
but maybe it gives it a thrill
like maybe meeting you
would be a liberating pill

I like the quiet sometimes
just hold me while you wait
kiss me slow and soft
ask me to be your valentine date

I've never been anyone's valentine
honestly i don't know what people do
they meet and just love each other
but us? what would we go through?

So reassure me once
or as many times as you please
I know it might feel like a burden
but it's something i really need

I love valentines
or maybe the idea of it
its just the thought of being with you
doing things I'll never admit

I don't need the grand gestures
just talking to you is perfect
hearing the sound of your laugh
makes me feel like I'm looking at a golden sunset

11. Longing

I just want to be loved
loved like I'm precious
like someone wouldn't survive,
if I didn't exist, he'd be grievous

I don't want to be the two oceans that met
but never mixed
like no matter how hard we tried
fate's never fixed

Everyone loves me
but no one has ever been in love
they all say they care
but I'm just not enough

I question myself
if I am that unlovable really
I don't say it out loud
if I did, they would see the real me

I make jokes about
the things I seriously care
because if I talked about it
I'd just gain another glare

What is wrong with me?
I don't know
maybe I talk too much
or maybe I'm just for show

So all I want is to be loved
to actually matter to someone
to be hugged tight
to be with someone for the long run

12. Eternity

You keep making excuses
about how hard it is to write
so i gave myself a little challenge
to write about you tonight

I could write novels about your smile
and it still wouldn't be enough
it is magnificent, so when you say
you don't like it, I call your bluff

Its true, it makes me feel
so many things at once
you asked why i liked you
if only I could say what i wanted to for months

But i can't, So I write instead
your smile is the epitome of the dark
people could see and go
but for me, it leaves a permanent mark

A mark, i never want gone
I want it forever
it makes the days i dread
so much better

It might sound clichéd
but it gives me butterflies
it makes me want to believe
everything you say, even if they're all lies

You ask me why i trust you
its just something you do
I can't help but fall
your smile reminding me of the spring dew

Its rare but its perfect
I could stare at it for all eternity
its a promise,
even if you think of it as absurdity

13. Enchanting

I was drawing the dream guy
I would give my heart to
but somehow the drawings
look a lot like you

With the charm so bright
you shine in my eyes
its like you're the inspiration
for all the fictional guys

You're the best
no matter whoever I'm shown
and your smile just proves that
nothing i write is wrong

You are magical
to laugh with and talk
but I would spend hours with you
even if we're on a silent walk

Enchanting
that's what you are
I'm not talking about physical appearance
though if i did, I don't think I would make it very far

I think your voice
it puts the best music to shame
if anyone asked my favourite song
I wouldn't hesitate to take your name

"Write about something better"
but I can't think of anything that is
I know I'm not good but
writing about you, is a chance i don't want to miss

If love was a person
it would hug you tight
feel your presence
and relish in your shining light

Its a bit silly I guess
but i wish on every shooting star
that I want to be the light
when you feel lost in the dark

14. Yearning

I miss you
I don't know if it's right
I want to hug you
just hold onto you tight

I look at you
and I see the end
but we never even began
we were after all just friends

I can't lose you
I love you too much
but I don't think you would believe me
even after we lose touch

I haven't even met you
and I fell so fast
I write you poems because
I still believe that we could last

I want you to hold me
let me cry in your arms
I can't keep doing this anymore
I'm not immune to your charms

You're good at everything
from academics to creativity
I would spend days and hours
admiring your smallest activities

You're mesmerizing
no words are ever enough
every flaw you have is
just proof of you being so tough

15. Ghosts

You're goofy and I love it
I couldn't say it better
you're like the sun
and you don't know how much you matter

You make want to write
letters, to you and to world
just saying how amazing you are
that I'd meet you in the after world

We'd be ghosts
but be close
we'd meet everyday and
I'd be glad its you i chose

But to be ghosts
we don't have to die
we could just be haunted
by our memories till we cry

But maybe only I would
because you still aren't sure
it's been 5 months but
you don't believe my feelings are pure

You make me happy
more than anyone has ever before
and it's kind of funny, you're not even mine
but you're the one person I would live and die for

That's why, I'll be the ghost
and I'll come to your home
we would laugh together
and live our dreams without the fear of being left alone

16. Daydream

He's a daydream,
so familiar yet far,
like tracing constellations
that never quite are

She thinks of him every second,
a wish on repeat,
hoping one day
their hearts finally meet

The distance is vast
yet he's always so near
a dream she keeps chasing
a voice so clear

She thinks of him every second
like lyrics to a song
a rhythm in her heartbeat
playing all day long

Then she wonders if he feels it
if his mind drifts away too
if in a quiet moment
he's dreaming of her too

But the thing about dreams
is that they fade too fast
she reaches out to hold him
but daydreams never last

17. Almost

He almost said it
the keyword being almost
words stuck on his tongue
a whisper, dangerously close

A pause, a hesitation,
his heartbeat fast
fear holding him back
as the moment just passed

She felt it lingering
hanging in the air, unsaid
in the way he stopped
with a shake of his head

He was fighting
against every fear, against fate
against every past scar
that told him to wait

She knew it all too well
she saw it in his eyes
in the way his gaze lingered
and the way he sighed

So she smiled like she didn't notice
laughed like she didn't mind,
deep down she always wondered
would almost ever become this time?

18. Red Light

Red is often associated with love
romanticised to a high post
but its also the colour of blood
leaving behind a haunted ghost

A ghost of memories
of heartbreak and a dark sky
they say roses are mystic
but just look at the petals dry

Inside a book,
a diary or a letter
its a reminder of
what could've been so much better

When its withered
the petals are wrinkled and brown
it had a loving memory
which, slowly, you watch drown

It drowns in a sea of emotions
what you could've done more
maybe they'd still be yours
if only you hadn't walked out the back door

You look at it and remember
everything you'd done wrong
red roses were their favourite
now it's just something to dread lifelong

Maybe your perspective is different
maybe you still believe their love
it helps you relive moments
which would've been best to be rid of

But at least you're happy
in red, you find the light
many see it as danger
but you find it a majestic sight

19. Right Person, Wrong Time

I have the purest intentions
and i think that's the worst part
there's no ulterior motive
just brutal honesty
breaking my own heart

You keep using it against me
saying that i shouldn't love you
but why don't you understand
that with you, I became the girl I once knew

You're so scared of hurting
but you said it yourself
that I'll stay unconditionally and
won't ever put you back on the shelf

I don't know how to love you
but to learn seems worth the try
and I know when you see this

you'll wonder "but why?"

I know you're hurting
when you push people away
but I met you to convince you
that sometimes, *they stay*

Some people want to
even when you're afraid
and I will never be ready
to let you take the blame

I knew this would happen
I always prepare for the worst
I tend to self sabotage
then think I must be cursed

There are always two options
I think you'll pick the second
to stay or to go
to go I reckon

Because you're so scared of being,
being in love, being lost
you're so scared of breaking
so you do the classic "hurt me till I'm gone"

It's not anything new
I've experienced it before
and I really thought that this time
you wouldn't walk out the door

I never said I'm a saint
I can't always be so understanding
why don't I get to feel the negatives
without the guilt stabbing

I know you care about me
at least I hope you do
but something in my mind
tells me it's all too good to be true

I want to ask you
why you feel this way
why you push me away
because I feel so confused
trying to figure what you say

But I don't know how
I feel restless when I question if you're mine
but I guess that's what we call
"Right person, Wrong time."

20. Inescapable

He said it
and she cried
he said he loved her
and all she wanted was to stop time

She had never cried
happy tears for a guy before
but that night, the stars
seemed to shine more

she read the words again
heart racing, unbelieving, unsure
still they remained there
steady and pure

She laughed through the tears
trembling, heart light
as if everything clicked into place
and feelings were set right

No grand gestures
nothing planned as a movie scene
just love in a message
real and keen

The screen glowed softly
a moment so small,
shifted her world
and changed it all

The miles stretched longer
both hours apart,
but his words reached her
like a balm to her heart

So many nights spent crying in bed
for so long she'd tried
now, at last,
he finally stood by her side

21. Whispered Hearts

I met this pretty boy
so pretty eyes, they're serene
sometimes they're brown
love in them as he speaks

He has locks of dark hair
that curl more than mine
and i feel so lucky
that i can call him mine

He's the perfect combination
like when its raining in the sun
he's the snow in December
and he might just be the one

Pretty boy is very tall
well, in comparison to me
and he has this mindset
that some people are just meant to be

I wonder who he thinks about
when he says stuff like that
and pretty boy is nervous
when he invites me to chat

I met this pretty boy
he's creative and quite funny
and he helps me calm down
when I'm drowning in worry

He never accepts the good in him
but i see it plenty
I keep telling him how perfect he is
hoping he doesn't feel empty

Dumb conversations
as he whispers out of the blue
I'm yapping and he says
"I Love You"

9 789369 530458